THE GREAT US AND BRITAIN BREAKUP

THE DECLARATION OF INDEPENDENCE

US History for Kids | Children's History Books

BABY PROFESSOR
EDUCATION KIDS

Speedy Publishing LLC
40 E. Main St. #1156
Newark, DE 19711
www.speedypublishing.com
Copyright 2017

All Rights reserved. No part of this book may be reproduced or used in any way or form or by any means whether electronic or mechanical, this means that you cannot record or photocopy any material ideas or tips that are provided in this book

In this book, we're going to talk about why the British colonies in America fought against the British to gain their independence and become the United States of America. So, let's get right to it!

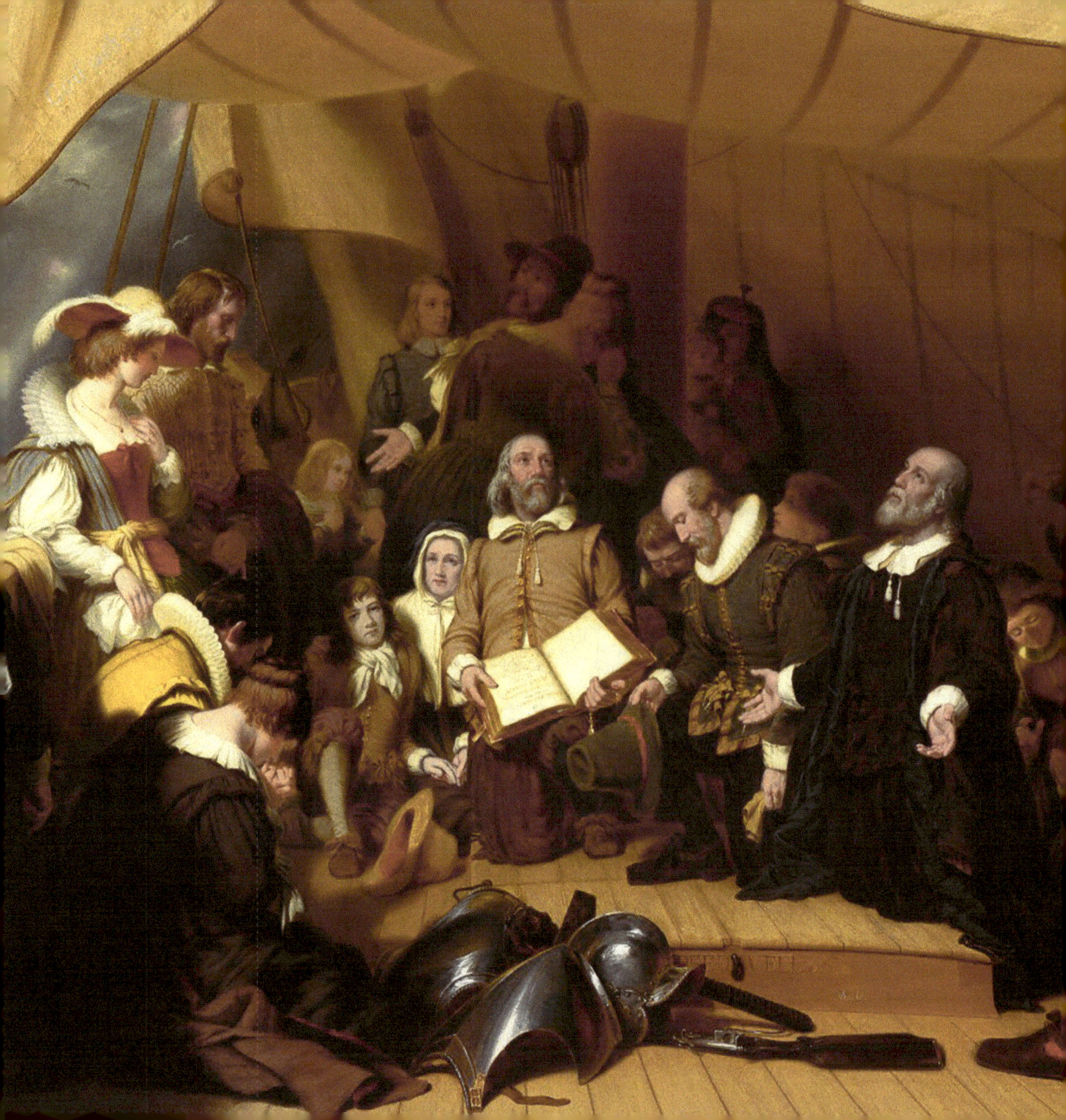

★ ★ ★

The earliest settlers came to America from England in 1620. They left England because they wanted religious freedom. It was very difficult to establish colonies in America. They had to build their own structures and plant their own food.

★ ★ ★

Many people died from diseases and surviving the harsh winter cold was a challenge. However, eventually the new colonies flourished. The colonies were part of Britain, but they had been self-ruling for over 150 years. Then things changed.

MAYFLOWER II

AMERICAN REVOLUTIONARY WAR

WHAT ACTIONS LED UP TO THE REVOLUTIONARY WAR?

★ ★ ★

When people rebel against a government, they usually have a long list of grievances before any violence occurs. The unrest with the colonists began after the French and Indian War.

THE FRENCH AND INDIAN WAR

★ ★ ★

The French and the British were at war in Europe. France and Britain were fighting in America too. The colonists and the British were one side and the French were on the other.

FRENCH AND INDIAN WAR

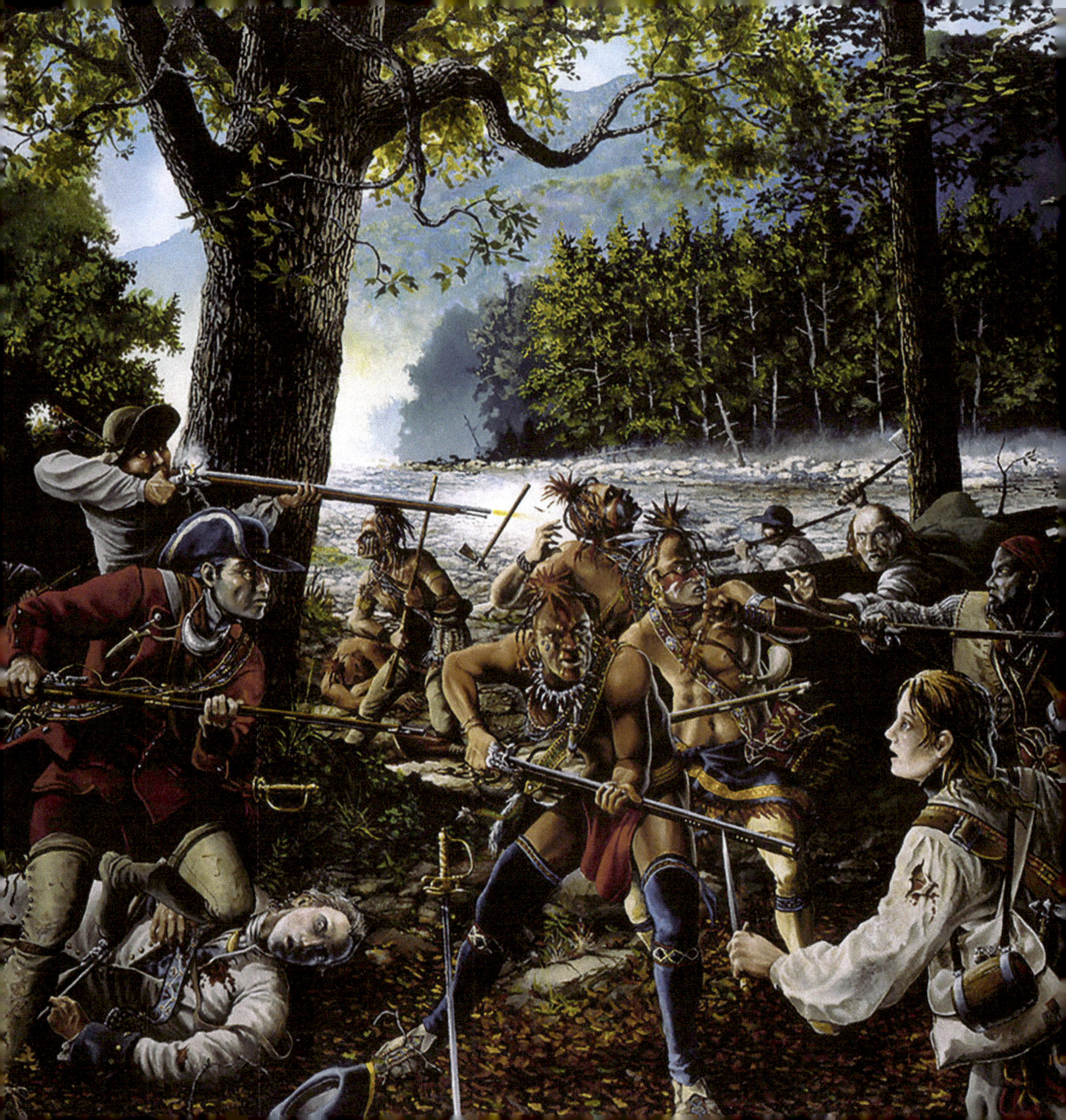

★ ★ ★

Native American tribes were split. Some sided with the British, some with the French. The war in Europe lasted a long time and Great Britain had a huge amount of debt when the war was over. Then the troubles began.

TAXES AND MORE TAXES

★ ★ ★

The British still had troops in the Americas. To pay for these troops they needed money and started to tax the colonists. First came the Sugar Act and the Currency Act followed by the Stamp Act of 1765. The Stamp Act meant that every sheet of paper was taxed. Legal documents and newspapers were taxed.

BURNING OF STAMP ACT

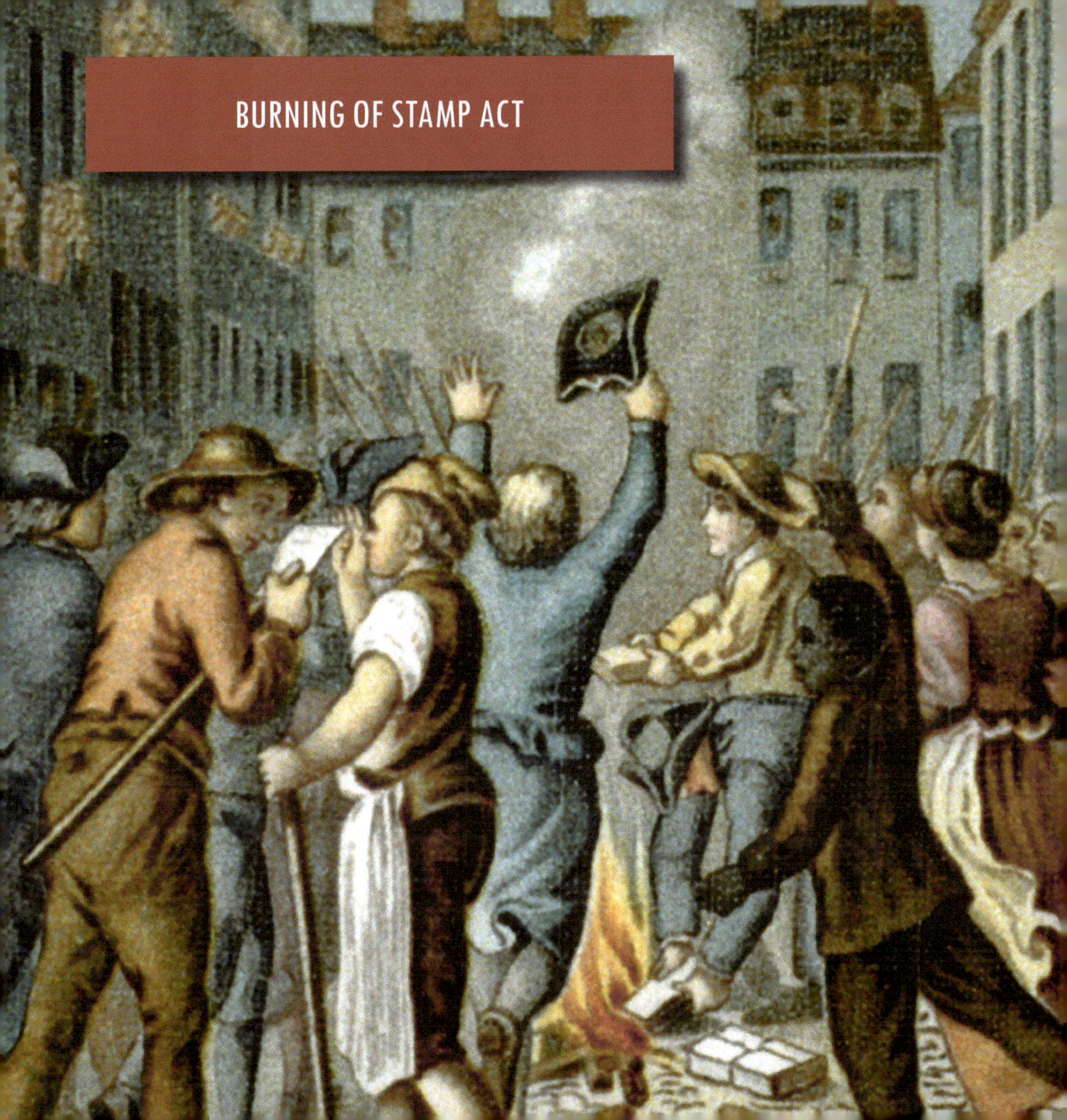

STAMP ACT RIOT IN BOSTON

★ ★ ★

Even playing cards were taxed. The colonists started to fight against these taxes and refused to pay them. After all, they had no say in what the king or Parliament decided. They agreed that there should be "no taxation without representation." More and more taxation laws were passed and the colonists got angrier and angrier.

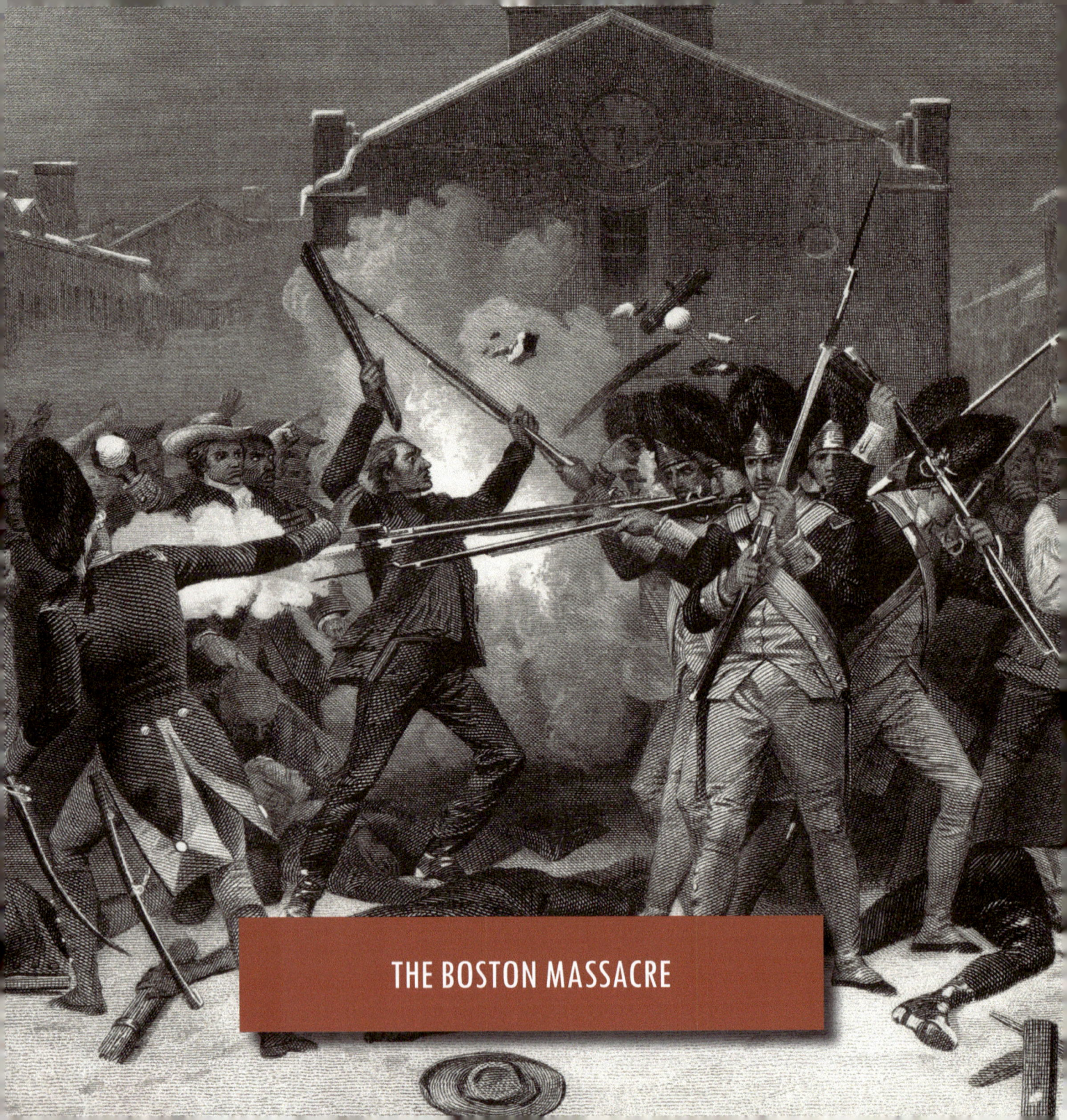

THE BOSTON MASSACRE

THE BOSTON MASSACRE

★ ★ ★

In 1770, in Boston, Massachusetts, a British officer who was unable to find suitable quarters for his soldiers had them pitch tents on Boston Common, which is the central plaza area in Boston. The soldiers were provoked and opened fire killing several colonists.

THE BOSTON TEA PARTY

★ ★ ★

Three years later, the British levied a new tax. This time it was on tea. Several Boston patriots protested the tax by dumping the tea off the ship. This event was called the "Boston Tea Party." The British responded by imposing even more punishing taxes.

DESTRUCTION OF TEA AT BOSTON HARBOR

BATTLE OF LEXINGTON

★ ★ ★

The American Revolution began on April 19, 1775, ten years after the Stamp Act, when fighting broke out between the British and the Patriots at the Battle of Lexington. The fight for independence had finally begun.

HOW LONG HAD THE COLONIES BEEN AT WAR WITH BRITAIN?

★ ★ ★

At the beginning, the unrest in the colonies was due to the fact that they were being taxed without any representation in Parliament. However, little by little, they began to dream of having their own country completely separate from Britain.

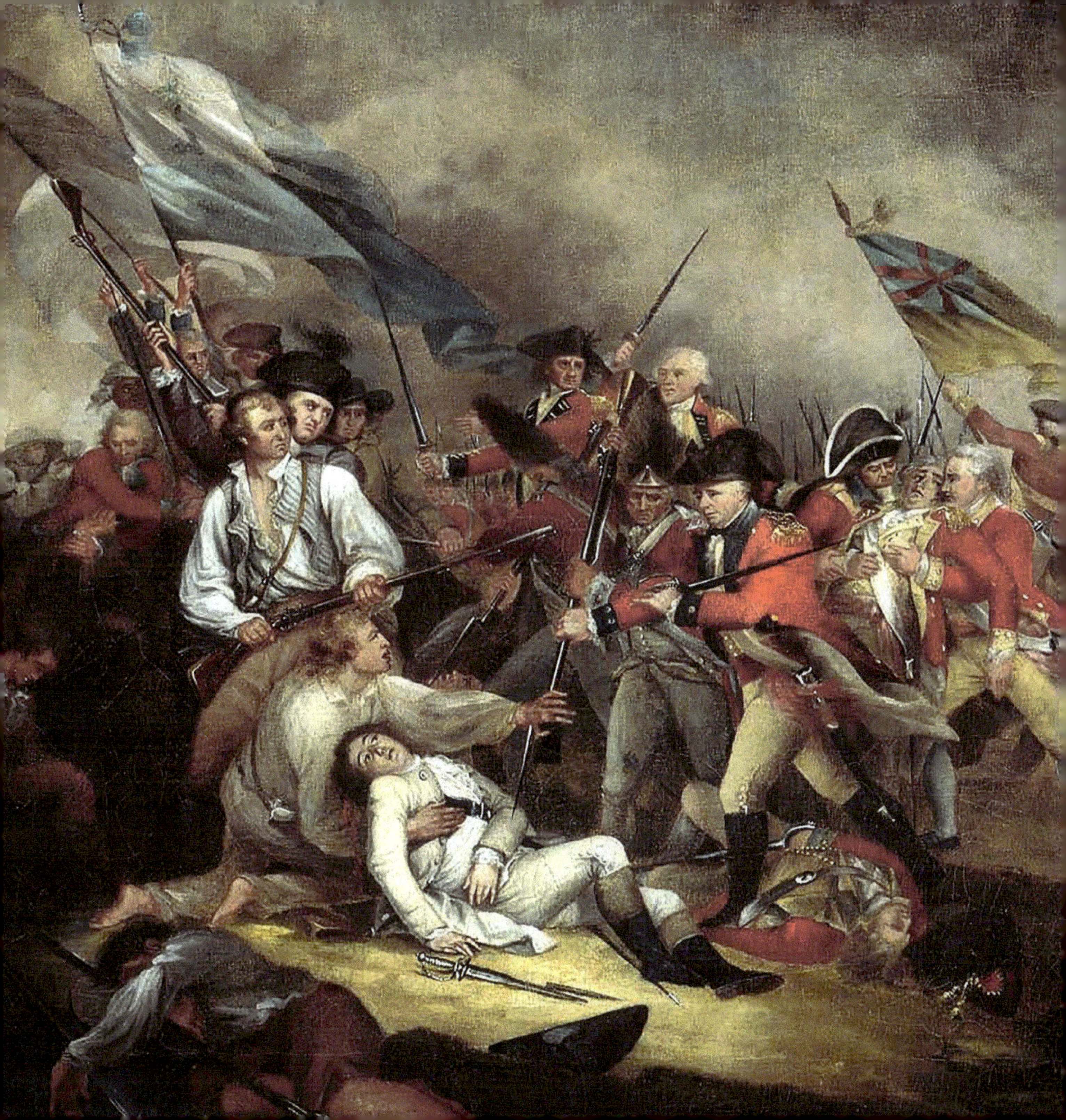

BATTLE OF BUNKER HILL

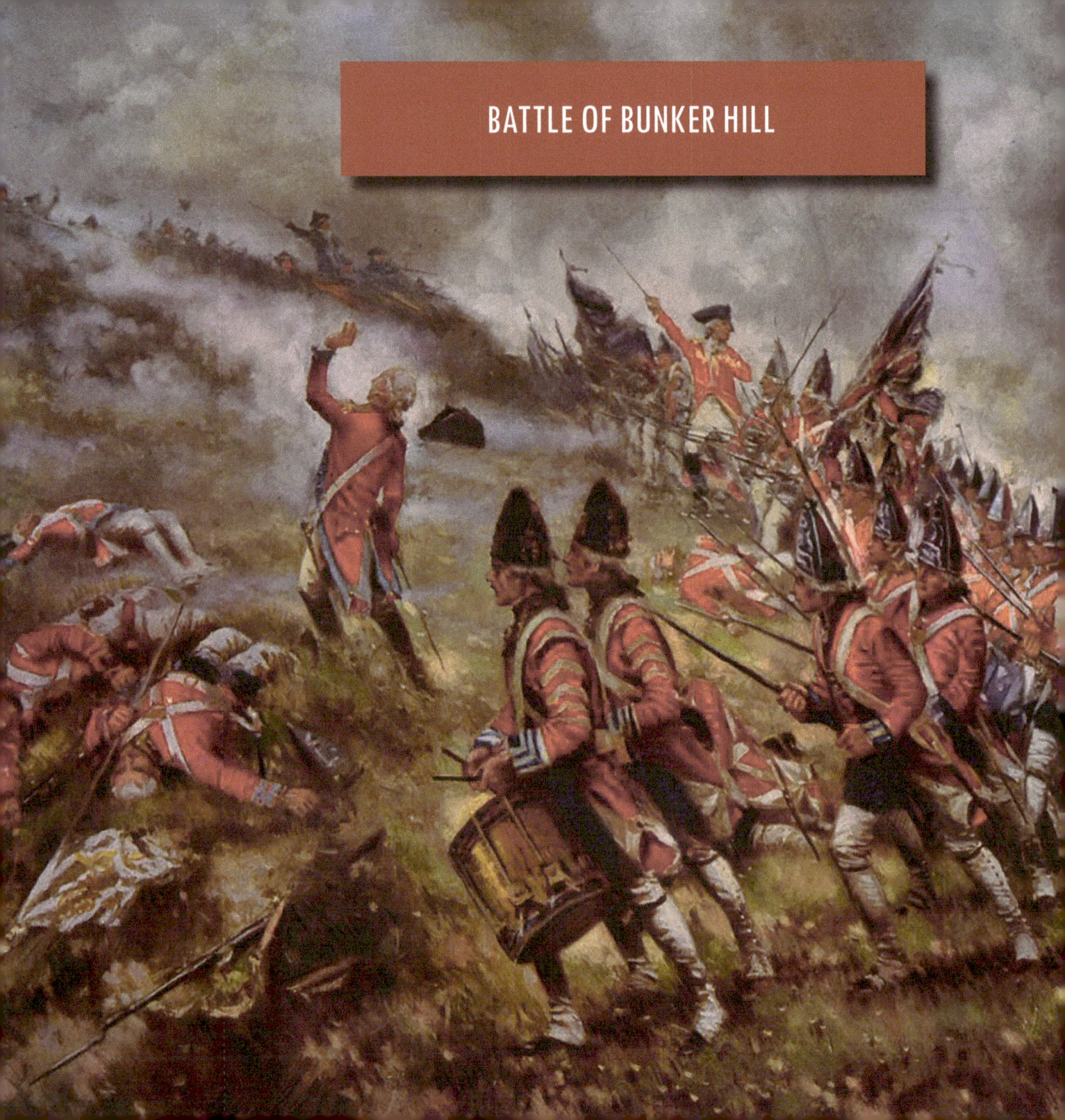

★ ★ ★

The fighting had been going on for a year before the Congress decided to send an official "breakup letter" to the king of England. They wanted it to be clear that they were fighting to win their freedom.

WHAT IS THE DECLARATION OF INDEPENDENCE?

★ ★ ★

The Declaration of Independence is a famous document. It's the document upon which the United States of America was begun. The document explained why the colonies wanted to be free of British rule. It explained the complaints that the colonies had with the king and the Parliament in blow-by-blow detail and outlined the philosophy behind the freedoms they wished to attain.

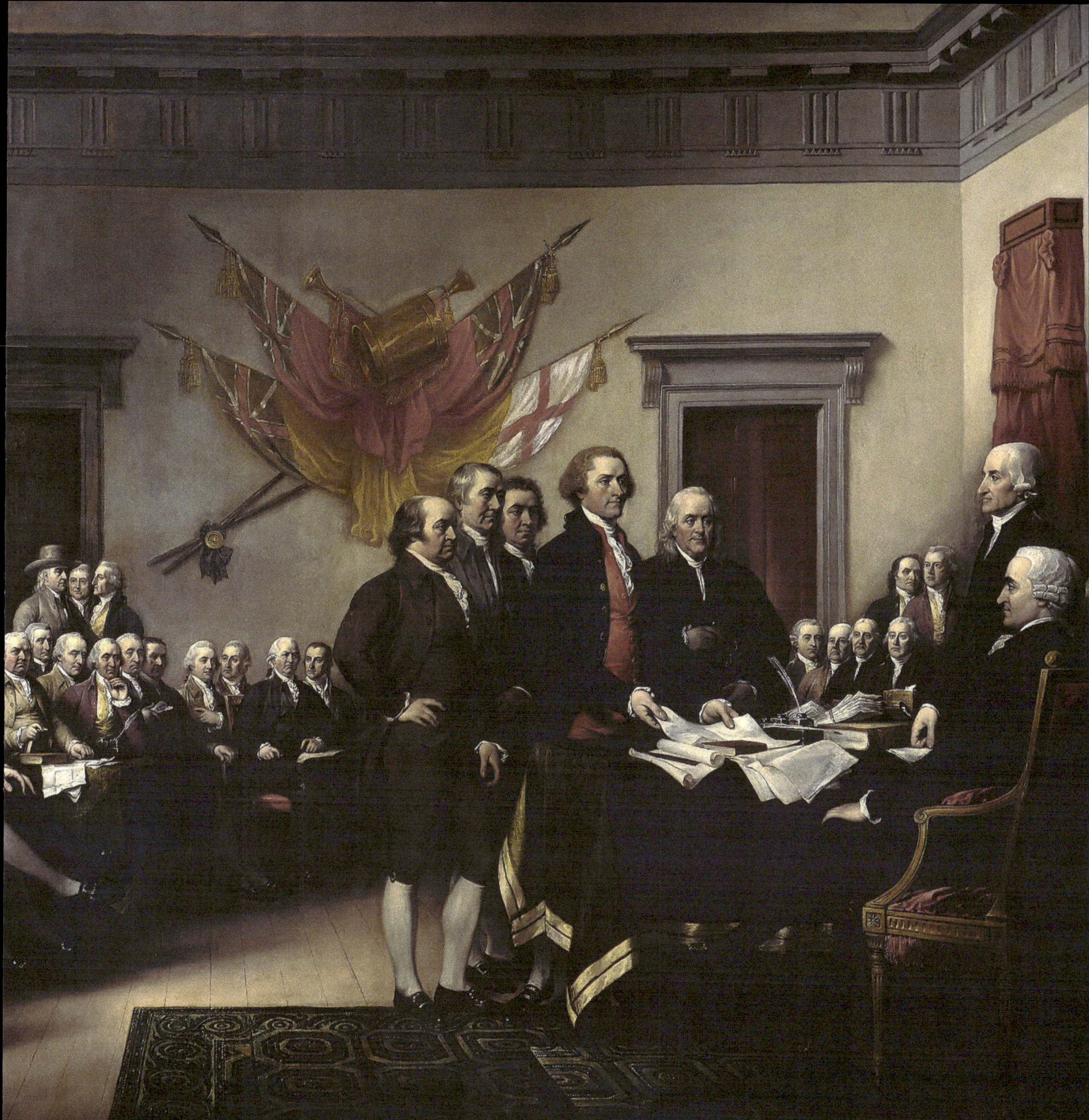

WRITING THE DECLARATION OF INDEPENDENCE

WHO WROTE THE DECLARATION OF INDEPENDENCE?

★ ★ ★

Like any document, it started with a first draft. On June 11, 1776, the Congress selected five important leaders from the group. Their task was to write the Declaration of Independence that would be sent to defy the king.

These men knew that if they lost the war they might be hung for treason. They were brave and believed strongly in the principles of freedom and equality for all.

The five men who met together to create the document were:

- ★ John Adams, who later became the second US President
- ★ Benjamin Franklin, who was a printer, a scientist, an inventor, and a diplomat
- ★ Robert Livingston, who was a lawyer and a diplomat
- ★ Roger Sherman, who was a lawyer and a statesman
- ★ Thomas Jefferson, who later became the third US President

DRAFTING OF THE DECLARATION OF INDEPENDENCE

THOMAS JEFFERSON

★ ★ ★

After they discussed what they wanted to include, they selected Jefferson to be the main author of the document. He composed the first draft within two weeks. Then they all met to make final amendments.

On June 28, 1776, they offered it to Congress for review.

DID ALL THE COLONIES AGREE TO THE DOCUMENT?

★ ★ ★

The colonies weren't in complete agreement that this was the right time to "breakup" with Great Britain. Some of the representatives wanted to give it some time.

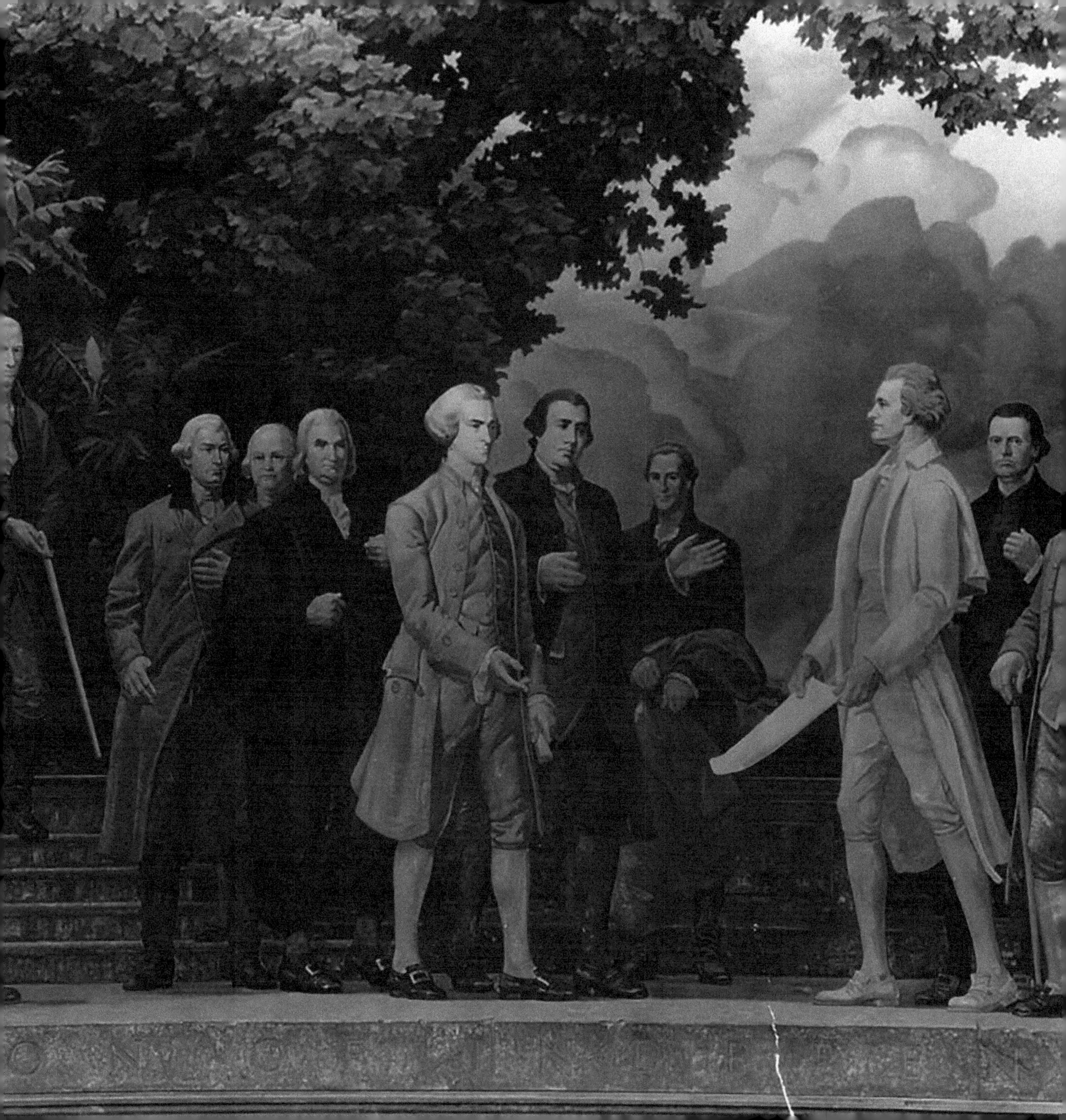

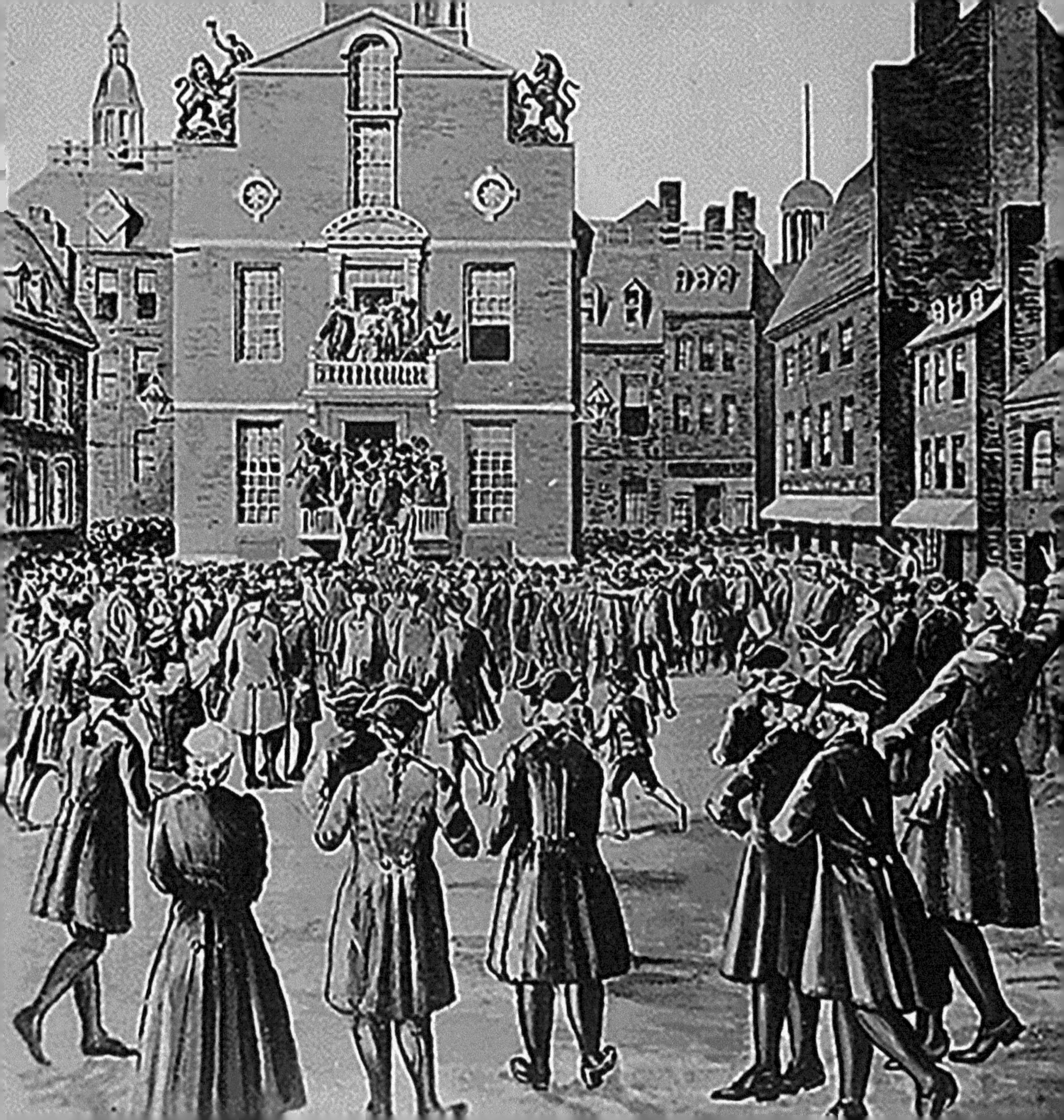

★ ★ ★

They wanted to line up strategic partnerships with other countries so that they had someone else on their side in the fight against Great Britain. New York and Delaware abstained from voting, which simply means they didn't cast a vote. South Carolina and Pennsylvania didn't say yes in the first round either.

★ ★ ★

The Congress as a whole felt strongly that the vote should be unanimous. Debate continued on the issues. As the debate wore on, the representatives from South Carolina as well as those from Pennsylvania changed their votes to yes. Delaware also cast its vote for yes. The only colony that chose not to vote was New York.

The Declaration of Independence had passed with a dozen "yes" votes.

INDEPENDENCE HALL ASSEMBLY ROOM

INDEPENDENCE HALL

INDEPENDENCE DAY

★ ★ ★

In the United States we celebrate the 4th of July as Independence Day because this was the day in 1776 that the final document was approved. It wasn't signed by the members of Congress until August 2nd of that same year.

FASCINATING FACTS ABOUT THE DECLARATION OF INDEPENDENCE

★ ★ ★

Once the document was written and also signed, the Congress asked a printer by the name of John Dunlap to create about 200 copies so they could be distributed to different individuals in the thirteen colonies. These copies were called the "Dunlap Broadsides."

DUNLAP BROADSIDE COPY

ROBERT LIVINGSTON

Only 26 of them have been found and are in collections. In 1989 a Dunlap Broadside was found and it sold at auction in 2000 for $8 million dollars.

One of the members of the writing committee, Robert Livingston, helped to draft its copy but never signed it because he believed the timing was too soon.

★ ★ ★

Thomas Jefferson was a gifted writer, but even his draft was subjected to edits. The members of the writing committee as well as Congress made over 80 changes to the document. They also edited it down by 25%. Jefferson was not pleased by some of the edits.

THOMAS JEFFERSON

GEORGE MASON

★ ★ ★

Jefferson was pressed for time in getting the Declaration ready so he relied heavily on the document for Virginia's Declaration of Rights, which was written by George Mason, a representative for Virginia. Ironically, Mason never signed the final Declaration of Independence. Jefferson also used a preamble to the Virginia Constitution that he himself had written for some of the wording.

★ ★ ★

In 1952, the formal copy of the Declaration of Independence plus the Constitution and the Bill of Rights were brought to the National Archives in the city of Washington, D.C. All three documents are on display there in the Rotunda that houses the Charters of Freedom. The formal copy of the Declaration is not the draft that was approved on July 4, 1776. The formal copy was signed on August 2, 1776.

ROTUNDA FOR THE CHARTERS OF FREEDOM AT NATIONAL ARCHIVES

JOHN ADAMS

★ ★ ★

The second US president, John Adams, and Thomas Jefferson, the third president both died on the 50 anniversary of July 4th. Only one signer lived past this date. It was one of Maryland's representatives, Charles Carroll. He was 95 when he passed away.

Nine of the men who signed the Declaration were no longer alive when the American Revolution was finally over in 1783.

JOHN HANCOCK

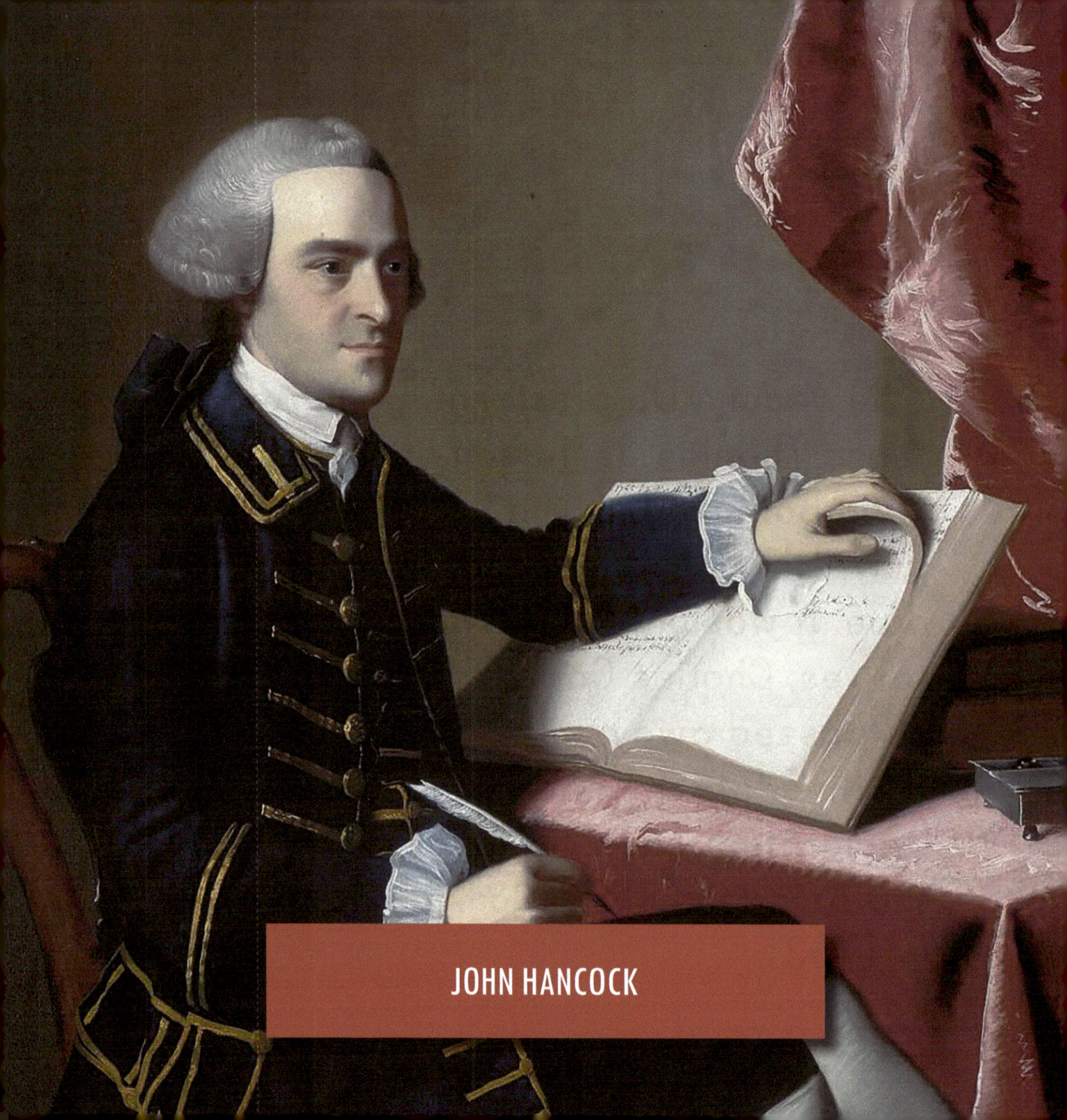

★ ★ ★

John Hancock signed his signature much larger than anyone else. He was president of Congress at that time and he signed first. Legend has it that he wanted his 5-inch wide signature to appear as large as possible so the king could read it without his spectacles. No one knows if this story is really true.

When the Declaration was signed in 1776, the US population was about 2.5 million people. Today the population of the US is over 300 million.

★ ★ ★

None of the signers of the Declaration were born in the United States, because the US didn't exist until the declaration was official. Eight of the fifty-six men who signed were born in the 13 colonies. The others were born in Europe.

ARCHIVES OF THE UNITED STATES OF AMERICA

NATIONAL ARCHIVES BUILDING

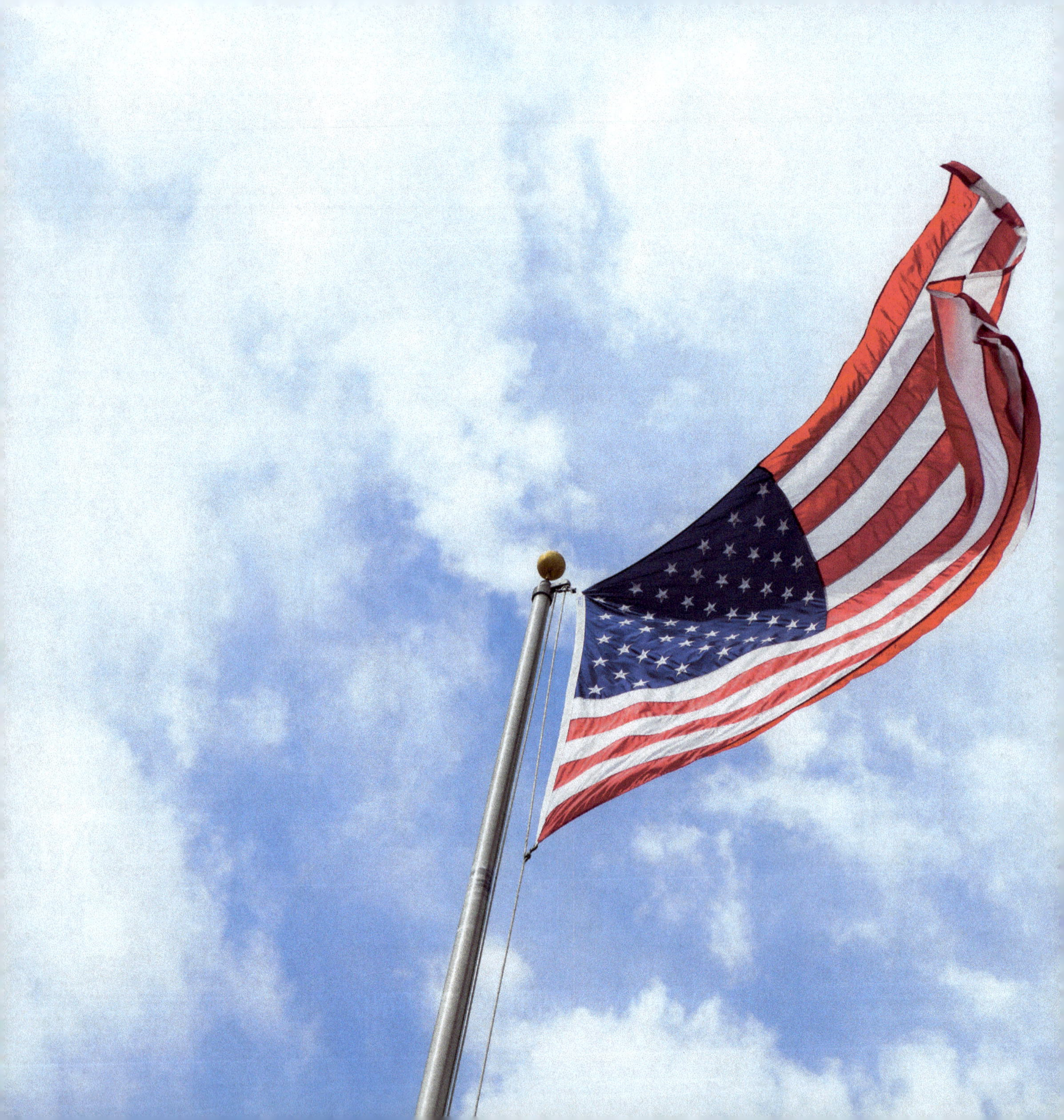

Awesome! Now you know more about the fight for America's independence and the Declaration of Independence. You can find more US History books from Baby Professor by searching the website of your favorite book retailer.

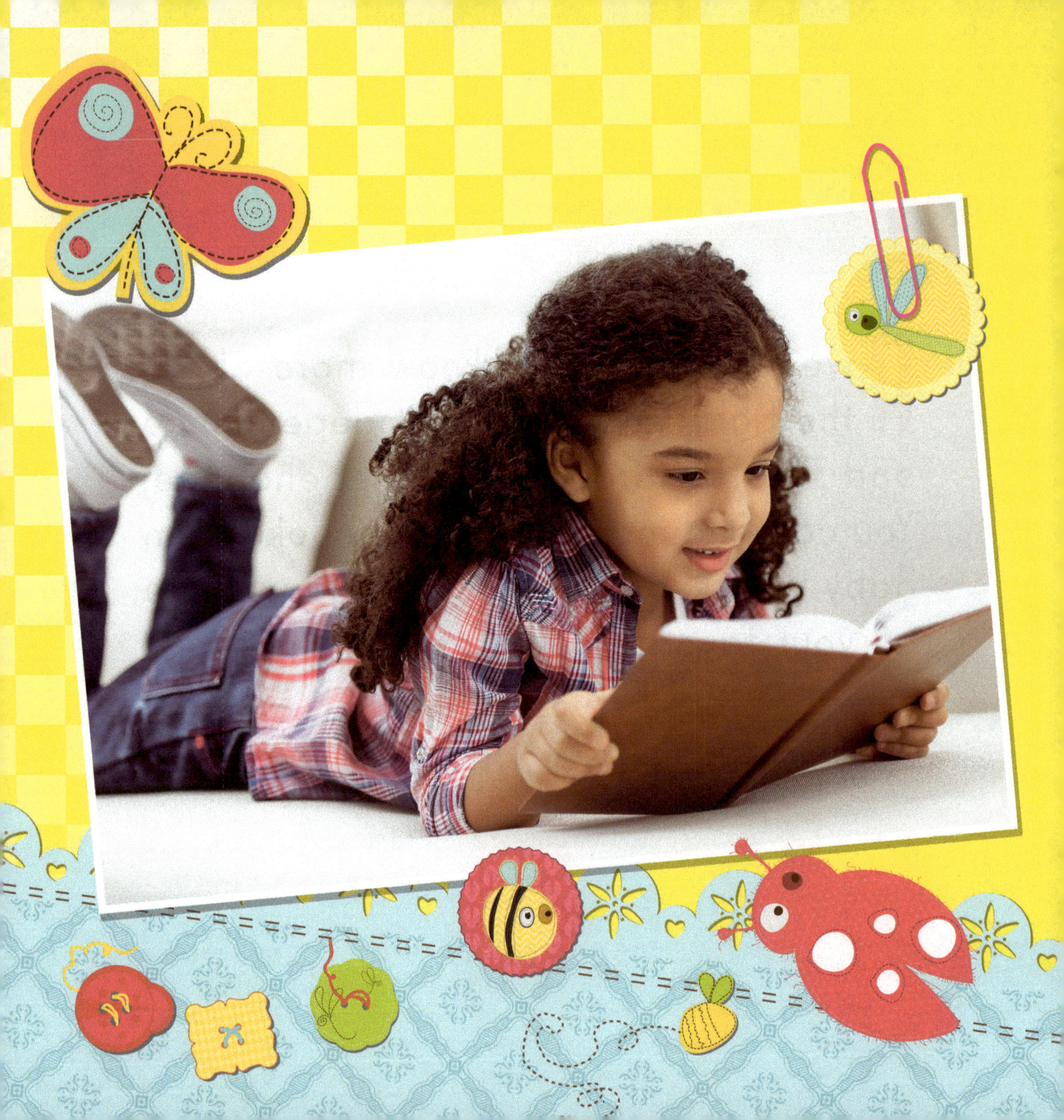

Visit

BABY PROFESSOR
EDUCATION KIDS

www.BabyProfessorBooks.com

to download Free Baby Professor eBooks
and view our catalog of new and exciting
Children's Books